Minimalism
A Beginner's Guide to Simplify Your Life

By Michael Lund

© 2014

Minimalism 101

Introduction

What is minimalism?

"Minimalism is a lifestyle that helps people question what things add value to their lives. By clearing the clutter from life's path, we can all make room for the most important aspects of life: health, relationships, passion, growth, and contribution." - http://www.theminimalists.com

If you thought that minimalism was all about white walls and no furniture, giving up all of your possessions and living like a monk, think again. The minimalist lifestyle is about much more than interior design.

In the United States, and other countries in the West, more and more people are choosing to live with less. This may mean having uncluttered living spaces or getting rid of certain possessions that you don't really need. But, as the quote above emphasizes, minimalism is much more than that. At its core, it is really about a way of life dedicated to the things that bring us most happiness and a renewed focus on those important things in life.

Many of the people who choose to live a minimalist life believe that materialism has failed to deliver on the promise of improving people's lives. Against materialism they offer minimalism as an alternative lifestyle choice.

But what is minimalism? (The *what?* of minimalism is straightforward. It is the *how?* that is difficult.)

The central idea of minimalism is to live without 'needless stuff.' 'Needless' describes anything that you don't use or does not bring value to your life. 'Stuff' can refer to possessions, activities, tasks or even relationships.

Minimalists do not always agree what exactly constitutes 'needless stuff.' Most would agree that the VHS video recorder rusting in the back of your garage is needless stuff. For many, a photo album you haven't looked at for ten years is also needless stuff. But is the garage itself needless stuff? What about the car?

However they define the movement for themselves, minimalists are usually clear on four principles: Firstly, we all have needless stuff. Secondly, only *we* can really decide which of the things we have is needless. Thirdly, once we have identified which stuff is needless, it must be removed from our lives. And lastly, we need to stop buying more of it.

These principles raise those *how* questions: How much needless stuff do we have? How do we decide if it is needless? How do we remove it? Luckily, minimalists have advice to help us with these how questions. We will cover this advice later.

Many people are put off minimalism by their preconceptions. So, firstly, let's look at the myths about minimalism.

What Minimalism is Not

There are many different types of minimalism, just as there are many types of minimalist people. There is no right or wrong way to live a minimalist life, only the best way for you.

A common misconception is that minimalism involves a road to Damascus epiphany. You need to change your life over night. Nothing could be further from the truth! Instead of one grand, abrupt change, minimalists emphasize that changing your lifestyle is a slow process, in which you gradually shed possessions and learn to live a more streamlined life.

It is true that for some people, minimalism echoes aspects of religion. It is common for religion to warn of the dangers inherent in material possessions. Despite this, minimalism has little in common with religion for the majority of minimalists. Think of it as something outside of religion. Think of it as a life philosophy.

Outright rejection of materialism is often associated with 'new-age' spiritualism – an individual approach to religious practices, often with a blend of Eastern religions thrown in. Minimalists are often at great pains to distance themselves from any 'hippie' stereotype. Becoming a minimalist does not entail switching to a lentil-only diet, wearing loose fitting clothing or sitting cross-legged.

Minimalism is not just about re-organizing your closet. Although this is useful, a shift to minimalism starts more fundamentally with a mental shift, and a change in your priorities.

Minimalists don't spend any money. This is a commonly held idea from others. This is certainly not true. Minimalists, like everyone else, spend money. Of course they do! But they do so carefully, only buying the things that matter most to them. They do not believe their lives can be improved by spending money. Typically minimalists spend money when they have to. Groceries? Good expense. A new smart phone? Not usually a necessary expense.

Another misconception is that minimalists live with only 100 things. This has become a popular belief, partly because people like to quantify things and 100 is a nice label to stick on minimalism, and partly because a few minimalists who do stick to a specific number of possessions. Dave Michael Bruno's '100 Thing Challenge' (100TC) has caught the imagination. But the number of possessions here is arbitrary and is merely a means to an end. To focus on the number is to miss the rest of the important idea.

Bruno describes his minimalism as "a way to personalize my efforts to fight American-style consumerism." In this, minimalists are often associated with opponents of materialism, including environmentalists and social activists.

There is an environmental reason to reduce of a demand on resources. Materialism, it is pointed out, is simply unsustainable. We have enough resources to meet our needs, but not enough to meet our wants. However, this is very much a side benefit of minimalism. It is not its main aim and any overlap with environmentalism is more coincidental than meaningful.

Minimalism is not a political or protest movement. It has nothing to do with political parties or processes. Advocates of minimalism talk almost exclusively about individual choices. They are only concerned with how consumer culture affects their lives.

Adopting a more minimalist lifestyle does not necessitate changing anything about your job, your hobbies, your diet, or your relationship with your family and friends. It is simply about having less stuff and enjoying the benefits.

Who is it Good For?

Minimalism can be adopted by anyone. Minimalists vary greatly in their approach to living with less. Some are fervent minimalists, committed to living a life with as few possessions as possible. Some are travelers who move from place to place living out of one bag. Some minimalists live alone. Others are married with large families. Some give up their cars and downsize to a smaller house. Others stay where they are and drive every day. Some work from home and grow their own food. Others keep doing the same job and shop at a supermarket.

There is not one typical type of minimalist and not one type of person who minimalism is good for. Most are simply trying to reduce the amount stuff they own to free up time and space.

The great advantage is that it is something you can try out, it is easy, simple to do and it doesn't cost you any money. You may find that certain aspects of minimalism appeal to you and fit with your life and you may find that other aspects are simply impossible in your current life situation. That is perfectly fine! Minimalism doesn't have to be an "all or nothing" idea. You can use the concepts and teachings of minimalism in whatever aspects of your life you can. You don't need to do every single thing that minimalists recommend. Even by changing one aspect of your life, you can positively enhance your day-to-day situation and take steps towards a better path. Start small and you'll see the changes that are possible with minimalism.

Benefits of Minimalism

The proponents of minimalism claim that, despite being a simple idea, the benefits are enormous. They claim minimalism improves health, finances and family life. It can help clear their minds and allow them to live more productive and enjoyable lives.

Dave Michael Bruno may have been trying to avoid the pitfalls of materialism, but he found minimalism brought "a life of simplicity, characterized by joyfulness and thoughtfulness."

Benefits to Happiness

Bruno is not alone in expressing these sentiments. Minimalists emphasize again and again that this lifestyle makes them happier. Why should this be?

Minimalists give two main reasons for this: Firstly, many are convinced that modern materialism makes us unhappy and removing ourselves from consumer culture can substantially improve our lives.

Materialism has brought us many more things than were available to previous generations. But it is stained with greed and lacks any real value other than the pleasure gained from purely consuming. To many it seems an unattractive way to behave.

This was evident in the excesses of last year's Black Friday. It was estimated that over 140 million Americans went shopping over that holiday weekend alone. In the UK Visa predicted shoppers would spend £518 million online on their credit cards.

Those who shopped online were probably wise as, according to the BBC, Greater Manchester Police arrested three men and a woman was hit by a falling television. The deputy chief constable of Greater Manchester Police described shoppers' behavior as "appalling." Black Friday was described as "the day we trample people for things we don't need, the day after being thankful for what we have."

With Black Friday followed rapidly by the Christmas shopping spree and the January Sales, it is little wonder there is growing weariness with relentless consumerism. The things we buy are not things we actually need and this lifestyle is not one we have chosen. Author Seth Godin observed, "Black Friday is a media trap, an orchestrated mass hallucination based on herd dynamics and the media cycle."

The psychological implications of this manipulation are damaging. A paper, published in *Psychological Science*, found that people repeatedly exposed to messages designed to target them as consumers, had an immediate increase in material aspirations, depression and anxiety. They became more selfish and competitive, and their sense social responsibility was reduced. Materialism clearly has psychological downsides.

In Iceland after the economic collapse, researchers found that individuals who focused on materialism, in the hope of regaining their previous status, reported lower levels of wellbeing. In contrast, those less interested in money, and more concerned with family and community life reported higher levels.

The minimalists' second argument is that needless stuff blights our lives. This is not simply the irritation caused by the fact the wardrobe door won't shut, the garage is overflowing and we can never find anything, but because possessions have little effect on their owner's well being. Minimalists contend we are making a terrible mistake in believing more stuff improves our lives. All it does is fill our houses with things we don't need.

This is the paradox of materialism, it promises happiness, but never delivers. It keeps us suspended in a permanent state of frustration, always one purchase away from feeling happy. Working to buy these things leaves us busy and stressed and we miss out on what is truly meaningful in life.

Most minimalists recognize that money can buy a degree of happiness, it depends how you spend it. The key is to choose to buy with care. Excessive consumption over any length of time makes you less happy rather than more.

Joshua Becket of the Becoming Minimalist website puts it like this:

> *"It is time to take a step back and realize that excessive consumption is not delivering on its promise to provide happiness and fulfillment. Consumption is necessary, but excessive consumption is not. And life can be better lived (and more enjoyed) by intentionally rejecting it."*

Benefits to Health

Our modern lifestyle exposes us to high levels of stress. A lot of the stress that is damaging our health arises from our inability to buy the things we have been persuaded that we need. Once we stop believing we need to buy so many things, the pressure is released. We are meant to be active, yet we often find that we spend our energies on things that don't make us feel healthy. Then we don't have the energy to do the things we would like to do. Minimalism reduces stress, encourages healthy activities and rebalances our diet. By living a simpler lifestyle we can improve our health and well-being.

Our modern materialist lifestyle encourages us to consume too much food and drink, too many artificial ingredients and over-the-counter medicines. The hectic lifestyle many people lead encourages them to eat fast, ready-made meals.

Most people would prefer to east healthily. Unfortunately, the food industry has used this desire to sell us more pre-packaged food under the guise of healthy eating. Often this is still full of chemicals and preservatives. It starts when we go shopping. The food industry is desperate to sell us more and more food that we don't actually want. Start by buying aware of what you buy and question whether you really need it.

Perhaps the worst example is manufactured vitamins. It makes no sense to consume things from a factory that copy what nature has already provided us. Minimalists try to eat simply and stick to natural, unprocessed foods.

This means eating more fruit and vegetables. Try eating a portion of vegetables with every meal and a portion of fruit between meals. These provide us with everything we need; they taste great and don't leave us feeling bloated and sluggish.

Be careful where you keep your food. If there is always food near you, you are more likely to eat it. TV encourages us to snack while we are minds are distracted.

Getting away from a materialist lifestyle will free up more time and energy to use for doing things that will make us feel better and improve our health. This shouldn't involve buying an expensive gym membership we will never use. Instead, enjoy activities in the fresh air with people you enjoy spending time with. These things make a big difference to our health.

Even if it is only for a short time, try to make exercise something you do every day. Once it becomes a habit you will find yourself sticking to it. A little and often is the best way to begin.

This may all sound like simple advice. Minimalists would answer that that is the point. There is nothing complicated or difficult about living a healthier life; we all know how to do it. If someone is making it seem complex they are probably trying to sell you something. The key is to start with small steps that slowly become permanent lifestyle changes.

Benefits to Your Wallet

One reason minimalism is particularly attractive now is that it fits with the age of austerity. After the economic collapse many people were forced to reassess priorities. With the price of goods rising quicker than wages, it is probably not surprising that people are questioning whether they really need so much.

In 2008 research by the polling group, Ipsos MORI, discovered that 20 per cent of British people agreed with the statement "I measure my success by the things I own". By 2013 this had fallen to just 16 per cent.

For many people it was not only all the needless things they had bought that were suffocating them, it was also the debt they had accumulated. This type of lifestyle is plainly unsustainable. Debt is stressful and stops people living their lives fully.

In order to lose their debt, minimalists downsize their living space, they say goodbye to their car and dumpsters full of possessions. Most are scared of doing this and worry about what this would mean for their standard of living. But all of them report the same thing – the feel freer, less stressed and happier about their future. Of course, their problems didn't all disappear, but it did give them the confidence to tackle them.

Benefits to the Family

One of the biggest complaints people have about modern life is that they never have enough time to spend with their family. When minimalists assess the benefits of their lifestyle, improving their family life is very often the biggest advantage. Minimalism frees up time and resources to spend on the things that are most important to you. But just as important, without pressure on your shoulders, the time you have is more productive and more enjoyable. Through minimalism, you can spend more time with the people you love, doing things that actually connect you as a family, and benefit everyone involved.

Often times, in our modern world, family bonds become strained and stressed, as everyone is dealing with outside pressures, distractions, and problems. When we all get home after a long day, the children go straight to the television or video games, Mom or Dad tries to cook something or, more often, orders some food for the family. This is not a productive way to build family bonds and strengthen your love for one another. Through minimalism, you can entirely change all of this. Do things that matter to you as a family and you will all benefit from the minimalist experience.

De-Cluttering your home

Downsize your Living Space

For many minimalists the attraction of living with less is the mobility it gives them. But you don't need to be a free spirit to enjoy the advantages of not paying to rent floor space filled with stuff you don't use, or being tied to a mortgage for most of your working life.

Despite the fact the average American home has doubled in size since the 1950s, we are still running out of space. We have bought larger houses in order to fill them with things we don't use. In the UK there has been an amazing growth of self-storage companies. People are paying for extra spaces to store their excessive purchases.

Get Rid of Things You Don't Need or Use

In *Still Life with Woodpecker* (1980), the writer Tom Robbins stated, "Any half-awake materialist well knows - that which you hold holds you." John Ruskin similarly observed, ""Every increased possession loads us with a new weariness."

Too much clutter suffocates and weariness comes from the constant battle to have a tidy home. To rid ourselves of possession-related weariness is the goal of minimalism. Success is measured by the amount of clutter we can remove from our homes. Again, it might seem a simple philosophy to enact – just put your unwanted stuff in the trash. But stuff has an ability to cling, limpet-like, to our homes. Many feel afraid to declutter, and it is easy to keep possessions for a while longer. Clutter symbolizes procrastination - the physical manifestation of our inability to organize our lives as we wish.

Tips

Some minimalists, like Joshua Becket of Becoming Minimalist, attack the problem all at once and get rid everything they don't need in a weekend:

"Three years ago, we sold, donated, or discarded over 70% of our family's possessions. We removed clothes, furniture, decorations, cookware, tools, books, toys, plus anything else we could find in our home that was not immediately useful or beautiful. The result has been a completely transformed life and lifestyle. It is a decision we have never regretted."

But for most people shedding stuff takes time and they need to be patient. Colleen Madsen at '365 Less Things' tries to give away one item each day. Another idea is to put four boxes in a room: trash, give away, keep, or relocate. No item is passed over. Each must be placed in one of the boxes.

The following steps enable you to reduce the clutter in your home:

Step 1: One In, One Out - The first battle in the war on clutter is to learn how to stop buying new clutter. A simple principle is to follow the one in, one out rule. Remove old worn-out or broken items when you bring in their replacements.

Step 2: Be Ruthless When it's No Longer Useful - Even if you don't need to buy a new replacement, any item that no longer works properly or is no longer useful, should be dropped in the trash.

Step 3: The Right Number - One of the results of excessive materialism is that we end up having many things that are basically the same. Is it necessary to have a TV and a radio in every room? Open a drawer and see how many things you have that are exactly the same. To reduce your possessions put them into groups of similar things. Do you need three winter jackets?

Step 4: Deal With Clothing - The three winter jackets are a common problem. First, halt the shopping habit. Go thirty, sixty or ninety days without adding to your wardrobe. Set a monthly spending limit and avoid sales racks. Once your spending is curbed, open your wardrobe and realize you own too much clothing. Some of it has to go. Start with clothes you no longer wear. Oprah Winfrey recommends hanging all your clothes in the reverse direction. After you wear them, return to the closet facing the correct direction. After six months you can identify the clothes that you don't need.

In the long-run prioritize quality over quantity. If you stock your closet full of things you love, you will have less desire to add to it. Investing in timeless pieces ensures everything in your closet is needed.

Step 5: Would You Replace it? - Ask one question of each item you have – if it disappeared over night, would you pay to replace it? If the answer is no, it's a 'needless thing.'

Step 6: The Garage Holding Area - What if one day you need that needless thing? One compromise is to introduce a preliminary stage. Rather than put all your needless stuff straight in the trash, put it in boxes in the garage. When you need something, take it out. After 6 months you'll have taken out all that's important. Everything else in the box can be discarded.

Step 7: Deal With Emotional Attachment - The major obstacle to decluttering our homes is the emotional attachments we form to our possessions. Once we attach memories to things it's hard to let go. Minimalists point out that it is the memories themselves that are the important things, not the stuff that is associated with those memories. If the memory is important to you, you are unlikely to require an object to preserve it.

Creating a Minimalist Budget

What are the Necessities in Your Life?

Learn to distinguish between needs and wants. We need a roof over our head, food on the table and to feel safe. We want new clothes, a car and to travel. Minimalism does not mean not having any wants, but it helps to be aware that they are merely wants.

Many minimalists feel it's useful to have a target number of possessions to aim for. For some, the ideal is to like to strip down their possessions so they can be packed into one bag, stored in a few boxes or put into the back of a car. It doesn't really matter what the target is, as long as you have a strong idea of how you would like to declutter.

Some argue that setting a number of things or a volume that they need to be packed into is thinking about it in the wrong way. Instead, they emphasize utility. Stuff is only needless if you don't use it. The best way to think about your necessities is to monitor what you use. If you don't use a thing, it's useless.

What are the things you spend money on that you don't even need?

All minimalists follow the fundamental tenet of minimalism - to buy less. What could be so difficult about not buying things? Why not simply choose not to buy?

But it's not as simple as that. Firstly, materialism pervades into every aspect of our lives. It is ingrained in our aspirations of a house, a mortgage and things to fill it with. It is a central part of events like weddings, birthdays and Christmas.

And secondly, there is advertising. On zenhabits.net Leo Babauta calls advertising the "biggest obstacle to a wonderfully minimalist life," and the "insidious whisper of the bad angel of commerce." Minimalism is about considering carefully how we want to use our time, space and resources. Advertising bends our ear and encourages us to act on a whim.

Minimalism asks us to accept our space and time is limited. Advertising tells us not to worry about it and spend anyway. Buying one thing is designed to lead you into buying another. The lure of the bargain is tempting. Humans are susceptible to the temptation of getting something for less. Sales and special offers tempt us to buy more than we need. Cheap consumer goods should mean we buy the things we need and save money. Instead, marketing convinces us to buy even more, and go into debt to do it. In 2002 the total credit debt in America was $660 billion. This had risen to $735 billion in 2005. Two years later the total consumer debt in America was $2.5 trillion.

Materialism rearranges our values. It encourages us to compare and compete with others buy more products. There is nothing new about this competitive edge to our buying habits. The phrase 'keeping up with the Jonses' comes from a comic strip by Arthur R. "Pop" Momand, first published in 1913. Since then it has become commonplace to measure social status and success by material goods. The material goods themselves become useless. We need to buy new clothes because other people are buying new clothes. We need a new model of cell phone because others are updating. Minimalists describe themselves as being in a race with everyone else and nobody feels like they're winning.

Tips

As with any budget make sure that your expenditure is less than your income. For minimalists the first stage is to establish what exactly you need each month and from that work out your monthly expenditure. We are used to believing that we need to earn as much as possible to cover all our costs, but that simply isn't true.

Your main aim should be to get on the pathway to removing yourself from debt. Most likely, debt will be accompanied by feelings of entrapment in a job and situation you dislike. A debt-free life is a life with freedom. Adam Baker from the website Man vs. Debt has lots of practical advice for escaping this.

One technique used by minimalist bloggers is to make their finances public and disclose on their websites all their expenses. This is an extreme way of making yourself think carefully about how you spend your money, but you can appreciate the rationale behind it

– if you have to justify your purchases to someone else, it might make them seem less essential.

Break down your expenses to 5 essentials:

1. Rent/Mortgage – Your largest expenditure and one that can't be avoided. Deal with this first.
2. Utility Bills – Everyone knows how awful it feels to be behind with bills.
3. Healthcare – Minimalism requires you to cut back your expenses. But its overall aim is to make you feel more at ease. This can't happen if you are worried about healthcare. Many minimalists choose their jobs in order to benefit from health insurance.
4. Food – You can't live without food and there is no need to bargain hunt. Buying good quality, healthy food will help you save money in the long-run.
5. Savings – It might be tempting to live hand-to-mouth, but that will not help your sense of well-being and it is almost inevitable you will need access to money at some point. If you do not have it, it will actually cost you more money to solve your problem. Top the fund up as soon as you have used it.

Here are 5 expenses you may not need:

1. Rent/Mortgage – It cannot be avoided, but does it really need to be so high? Is there another way to cut back on your costs?

This may also involve ridding yourself of utility bills and homeowner's insurance.

2. Car Payment/Insurance/Gas – For some people a car is essential, but for many it is a luxury that is draining their funds.

3. Cable TV – Takes up your time and your money.

4. Internet – If you only use the Internet where it is freely available, you use it more efficiently.

5. Credit Card/Student Loans – You can pay this off, the quicker you do so the more money you will save and the better you will feel.

Considering how to rid yourself of some of these big 5, added to your determination not to put more clothes in your wardrobe and more junk in your house, signals you have made a start on the road to minimalism.

Fun Activities for a Minimalist Life

For many people the most attractive benefit of a minimalist lifestyle is the extra free time. The problem then arises of how to enjoy this time without spending more money.

Minimalists believe life is better lived if you invest more in experiences and less in things. But marketing fuses experience and the object. We buy objects but have neither the time nor the money to enjoy the experience. Minimalism unpicks the confusion and focuses on what really matters: The traveler photographing amazing scenery – it is the vacation not the camera we want. The athlete running with the latest headphones – it is the exercise we need. The partygoer enjoying a night out – it is the event not the clothes you remember.

Materialism just points us towards shopping. We lose time for activities that make us who we are. Rather than real experiences we eat comfort food and watch box sets on the sofa.

There are countless activities we can participate in that, rather than encouraging us to buy something, give us experiences. The key is to form an attitude of curiosity and fun towards new experiences. Once you start you will find it becomes addictive.

For Singles

Approach the place you live with the mindset of a tourist. Most of us live for years in a place, never doing the things that tourists do in a week. If you feel that you live in a place that is not worth visiting, do a little research, the chances are you will be surprised to find how many things of interest are there. A good way to encourage this is to offer to show round a friend from out of town and let them reciprocate.

Take advantage of special offers on visitor attractions near where you live. Be aware of the special events happening near you. Often they look for volunteers and this is a great way to get involved.

Websites like Groupon and Living Social are useful ways to participate in a whole range of fun and unusual activities you might not ordinarily think of. Meetup helps you find interest groups in your area. You could have fun doing anything from cycling to exchanging recipes or playing chess. Another popular idea is language exchanges. You can help someone with a language they want to know and, in exchange, you can learn a language too.

For Families

It can often seem as if children are necessarily opposed to minimalism. They seem to make things a lot more complicated and require an enormous amount of stuff. In fact, they seem to require an enormous amount of new stuff quite regularly. This is probably untrue and it is adults who feel pressured into buying children a lot more stuff than they actually need.

What is certainly true is that children are not born materialists. If they ask for more and more things, it's because they have been taught to do so.

And children are definitely not natural born shoppers. If there is one thing they hate to do it is to go shopping. Children enjoy simple pleasures in life and give their parents continual pleasure that has nothing to do with buying more stuff.

The key to planning activities with children is not to plan too much with one activity after another. Be flexible. Enjoy the free time you have without creating a new schedule to replace the one you have opted out of.

Empty spaces on the calendar are chances for you to relax and really find out how your children enjoy spending their free time by letting them choose. Many parents impose their own busy lives onto their children by signing them up for after school clubs and sports. Children need downtime and to employ their own imagination to keep themselves entertained.

Fresh air and exercise are the things that children really enjoy and the things that are good for them, and these cost nothing at all. Children are always interested in nature, so any kind of nature walk or bug hunt capture their attention.

Minimalist Living Tips

A helping hand from technology

Technology has opened up the possibility of working, communicating, producing and being entertained whilst only using one or two small devices. All of the tools we used to need: paper, notebooks, pens, pencils, erasers, paperclips, staplers, and on and on, can all be tipped in the trash. With them can go surplus electronic equipment such as, calculators, DVD players, radios, TVs, home telephones, cameras and printers; followed by the redundant books, DVDs, CDs and photographed albums.

Minimalism is an idea of the Internet age and it is noticeable that, while minimalists advocate a life without many of the things most of us take for granted, they cling to their laptops and tablets. Little wonder, for these are the devices that make minimalism possible. The laptop is the perfect minimalist tool for work, leisure and a whole lifestyle. If the family gathered on the living room sofa watching TV, symbolized twentieth century consumerism, the minimalist with a laptop is a new era.

Minimalism is sometimes presented as a 'getting back' to essentials' or 'returning' to a simpler way of life.' But rather than giving up things, it is perhaps better to think of minimalism as the digitalization of our possessions. Instead of filling their homes, minimalists fill hard drives. It is a way of streamlining our lives to make the most of the technology available.

Letting Go and Being Grateful

Minimalism will Change Your Life

> *A minimalist lifestyle can have many legitimate*
> *motivations. Sanctimonious anti-consumerism isn't one*
> *of these, nor is saving money. – Sam Hughes*

As we have seen, minimalists talk a lot about saving money and perhaps even more about the dangers of materialism. Sam Hughes reminds us that neither of these are the really behind changing your lifestyle. Instead, minimalism is really inspired by your own change in values and a decision to take control of your life and pursue your own passions.

Minimalism is underpinned by a common sense idea and underlined by the obvious, practical improvements it has made in many people's lives and.

Change your mind

Albert Einstein said that, "Out of clutter, find simplicity. From discord, find harmony." According to minimalist theory, if you have found simplicity in your living space, you should also be moving from mental discord to harmony. Clearing surfaces and putting things away to create an uncluttered environment, provides people with a space to think and enables them to focus on what is important.

Physical clutter reproduces itself as clutter in our minds. Materialism directs our energies and interests towards things we can never attain. The result is that we are continually busy, and too stressed to spend time on what is important.

A minimalist lifestyle is really about redirecting our energy. Essentially, it is about learning to change our minds so that we can refocuses on what is most important and give ourselves the ability to control our priorities. Minimalists are advocates of 'single-tasking', believing that attention is best concentrated on one job are goal and only when it is complete, is it time to move on to the next.

Appreciate the little things in life

Omitting needless things is not only about material possessions, but about relationships, emotions, activities and actions. As well as removing physical things which have become a burden, you should look to eradicate those other burdens from your life: e-mails, to-do lists, action items, responsibilities, roles came about "one thing leads to another" when you let go of things.

There are a number of other steps you can take to improve the quality of your life and declutter your mind.

Step 1: Stop Being Busy - Being busy is almost a default. Not being busy suggests you are wasting time. But in itself, being busy is not achievement. Instead, consider whether you accomplish what you really want and if you spend your time doing what you like. If not, don't blame being busy. People choose to be busy. If you are too busy, you have planned badly.

To be less busy you need to plan your time to achieve your priorities. Don't make too many commitments. Omit needless activity by saying no to doing less important things.

Step 2: Focus - Minimalism encourages us to think clearly about what we would like to do. Firstly, it is necessary to discard inconsequential activities or goals. These are merely distractions. We should then decide what is really important and focus on just a few goals, or even one? By focusing on less, you can achieve more and make everything you do count. Look at your to-do list and see what's really important.

Step 3: Find Time for Things you Like - Reduce those activities we don't enjoy enables us to concentrate on those activities that matter most to us. For most people this means spending more time with family, friends, or pursuing their own passions. This begins to add up to a change of lifestyle. The quest for a life guided by passion is a meaningful life.

Conclusion

There are a large number of websites and blogs that provide much more information and guidance towards living a minimalist lifestyle. Here are just four you might want to explore:

- A blog that gives tips on living a minimalist lifestyle for those seemingly few minimalists in the UK - http://www.twolessthings.co.uk/

- Becoming Minimalist is designed to inspire others to pursue their greatest passions by owning fewer possessions - http://www.becomingminimalist.com/

- Uberless explores the multifaceted lifestyle known as minimalism, but with an added twist. It strips away all that is unnecessary and extraneous in my life, to make room for the things that bring joy and contentment. http://uberless.wordpress.com/

- Leo Babauta's Zen Habits is about finding simplicity in the daily chaos of our lives. It's about clearing the clutter so we can focus on what's important, create something amazing, find happiness - http://zenhabits.net

- Money Management and Tracking: the best site to track all your expenses (from what I can tell) is Mint.com. Mint helps you track your expenses and manage your money. It will categorize all transactions and enables you to set your budgets. All for free – http://mint.com

- Provides lots of great advice for saving money and rebalancing your finances. See the articles written by Joan Otto for some particularly good tips - http://manvsdebt.com/

There are also a great many books written on the same subject. Most are published as ebooks, so in the spirit of minimalism, you can download them to your Kindle and avoid overloading your shelves.

- *Essentialism: The Disciplined Pursuit of Less*, by Greg Mckeown involves doing less, but better, so you can make the highest possible contribution. – http://gregmckeown.com/
- *Stuffocation* by James Wallman is about how we've had enough of stuff and why you need experience more than ever. It is equal parts cultural commentary, trend forecast, and pick-and-mix menu of ideas for upgrading your life - http://stuffocation.org/
- *You Can Buy Happiness (and It's Cheap): How One Woman Radically Simplified Her Life and How You Can Too* by Tammy Strobel. Tammy Strobel and her husband are living the voluntary downsizing — or smart-sizing — dream and here she combines research on well-being with numerous real world examples to offer practical inspiration - http://www.rowdykittens.com/2012/03/you-can-buy-happiness-and-its-cheap/
- *Simplify: 7 Guiding Principles to Help Anyone Declutter Their Home and Life* by Joshua Bcker. Through personal stories, practical tips, and powerful inspiration, it provides

motivation for readers to live more life by owning fewer possessions. The book reminds us that life is too valuable to waste chasing possessions. It argues that each of us can experience practical, life-giving benefits by owning less - http://www.becomingminimalist.com/simplify/

*****

If you've enjoyed this book, PLEASE consider leaving a review and letting others know your thoughts. Thanks!

More books by Michael Lund:

The Lazy Investors' Guide: Save money. Retire early. The lazy way.

CPSIA information can be obtained at www.ICGtesting.com
Printed in the USA
LVOW10s1750260516

490118LV00021B/534/P